WORSHIP NOTES
&
ACTIVITY JOURNAL

AMANDA BALL-KNIGHT

WESTBOW
PRESS®
A DIVISION OF THOMAS NELSON
& ZONDERVAN

WestBow Press books may be ordered through booksellers or by contacting:

WestBow Press
A Division of Thomas Nelson & Zondervan
1663 Liberty Drive
Bloomington, IN 47403
www.westbowpress.com
844-714-3454

Scripture taken from the King James Version of the Bible.

ISBN: 978-1-6642-1384-5 (sc)

Library of Congress Control Number: 2020923076

Print information available on the last page.

WestBow Press rev. date: 01/11/2021

THIS BOOK BELONGS TO

_____

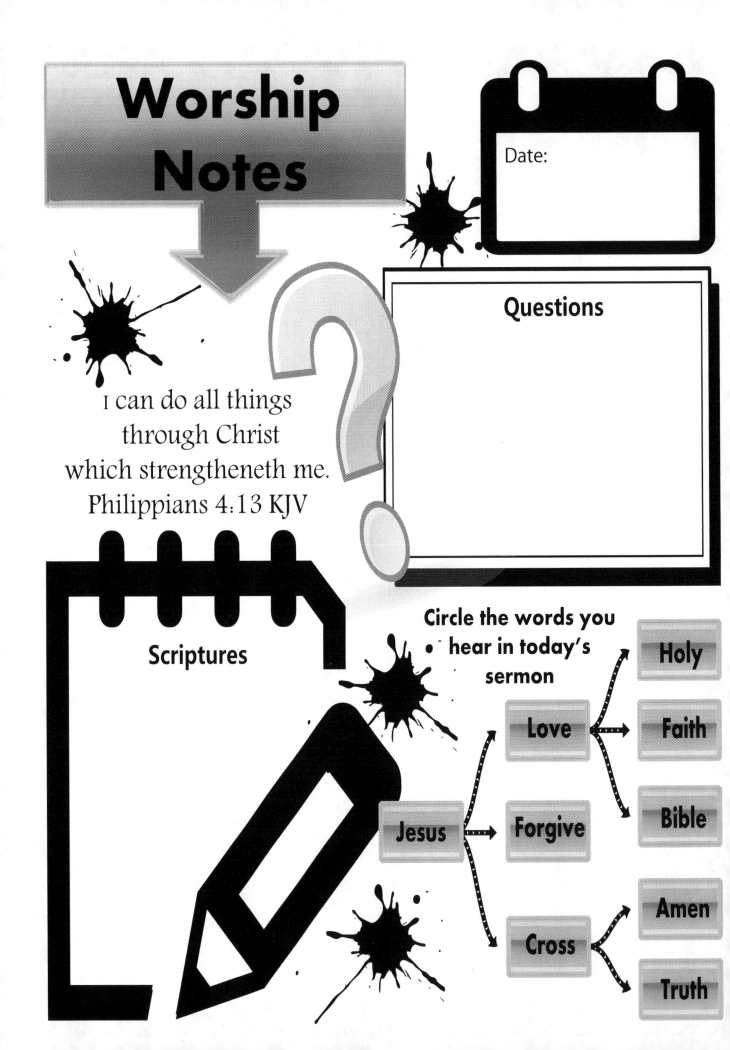

Color by Number

1- Yellow   2- Green   3- Red   4- Blue

Worship Notes

Scripture _____

Prayer Request _____

Questions _____

FAVORITE SONG FROM TODAY'S SERVICE

IN THE BEGINNING GOD CREATED THE HEAVEN AND THE EARTH. GENESIS 1:1 KJV

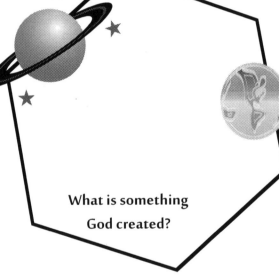

What is something God created?

DOODLE SPACE

HALLELUJAH

Write a description of today's sermon.

Colors of the Rainbow
Crossword Puzzle
Reference Scripture Genesis 9:12-17
God gave the RAINBOW as a promise.
Each missing word is one of the colors of the rainbow.

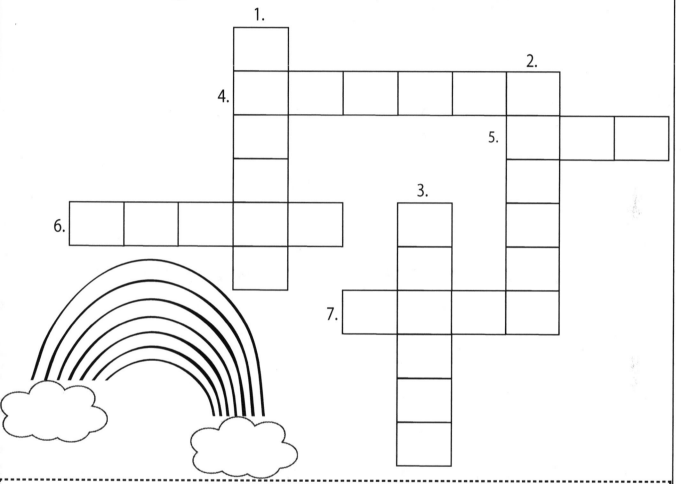

Down
1.) This color is a shade of purple.
2.) This is a fruit and a color.
3.) The color of a lemon.

Across
4.) This color is a shade of blue.
5.) The color most often used to symbolize love.
6.) The color of the grass.
7.) The color of the sky.

Word Bank
- Red
- Orange
- Yellow
- Green
- Blue
- Indigo
- Violet

WORSHIP NOTES

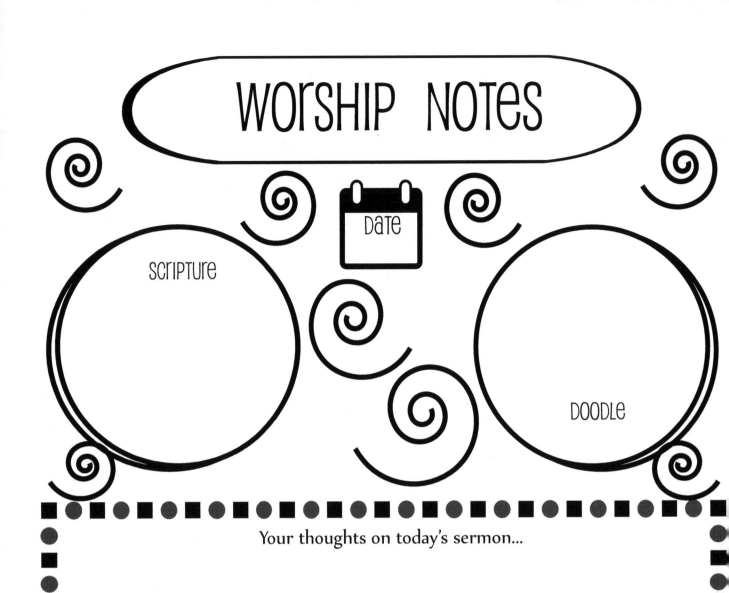

DATE

SCRIPTURE

DOODLE

Your thoughts on today's sermon...

SONGS

PRAYER REQUESTS

Travel through the maze to get to the Holy Bible.

"Trust in the Lord with all thine heart; and lean not unto thine own understanding. In all thy ways acknowledge him, and he shall direct thy paths."
Proverbs 3:5-6

Worship notes

Date: _____

Speaker: _____
_____

How can I use my hands
to be like Jesus?

Title: _____
_____

Scripture Reference: _____
_____
_____

Questions I have_____
_____
_____

For God so loved the
world, that he gave
his only begotten Son,
that whosoever
believeth in him should
not perish, but have
everlasting life.
John 3:16 KJV

Look up the Bible verse in your Bible
and fill in the missing words in the blanks provided.

We _____ him,
because he first _____ us.
1 John 4:19

And thou shalt _____ the Lord thy God with
all thine _____, and with all thy _____,
and with all thy _____.
Deuteronomy 6:5

_____ in the _____ alway: and
_____ I say, Rejoice.
Philippians 4:4

Worship Notes

Listen & Write

Words I didn't know: _____

_____

_____

Questions I have: _____

_____

_____

What I learned today: _____

_____

_____

Run to Jesus!
What can I pray for?

Today's

Date

PRAISE THE LORD

I did that!!
Circle the word that
you did in today's service.

Today's Sermon
is found.....
Book:
Chapter:
Verse(s):

Read

Clap

Say Amen

Sing

Pray

Stand

Raise your hand(s)

Praise

Listen

Draw a line from the number to what it represents.

For help you can read the refrence scripture.

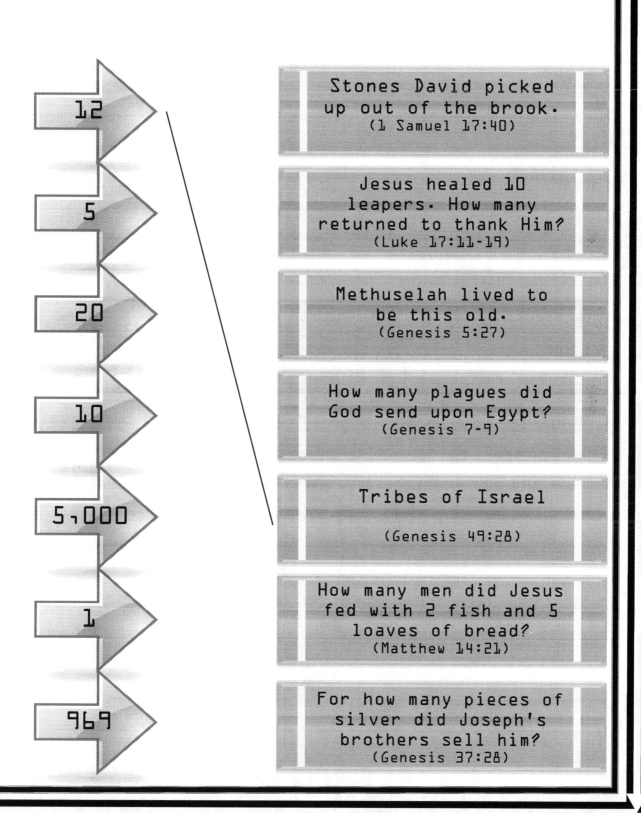

12

5

20

10

5,000

1

969

Stones David picked up out of the brook.
(1 Samuel 17:40)

Jesus healed 10 leapers. How many returned to thank Him?
(Luke 17:11-19)

Methuselah lived to be this old.
(Genesis 5:27)

How many plagues did God send upon Egypt?
(Genesis 7-9)

Tribes of Israel
(Genesis 49:28)

How many men did Jesus fed with 2 fish and 5 loaves of bread?
(Matthew 14:21)

For how many pieces of silver did Joseph's brothers sell him?
(Genesis 37:28)

God Made Me

Favorite Food

Favorite Hobby

Favorite Color

Draw a Self Portrait

My Friends

I'm a Star because...

My Family

Fill in the blanks using words from the word bank. For help look up each reference scripture in your Bible.

1.) Ishmael's mother, _____, was the handmaiden of Sarah. (Genesis 16:3-4)

2.) The city of _____ was built by Cain. (Genesis 4:17)

3.) _____ and _____ were known as the "Son's of Thunder." (Mark 3:17)

4.) Lazarus, a follower of Jesus, lived in the town of _____. (John 11:1)

5.) Isaac's mother was named _____. (Genesis 21:3)

6.) The Lord sent Jonah to preach in the city of _____. (Jonah 1:1-2)

7.) A man named _____ kneeled and prayed three times a day. (Daniel 6:10)

8.) Herod the great was king of _____. (Matthew 2:1)

9.) The staff of _____ became a serpent. (Exodus 4:2-4)

10.) A man named _____ built a temple for the Ark of the Covenant. (1 Kings 8:12; 17-21)

Word Bank

James	Solomon	John	Hagar	Moses	Nineveh
Bethany	Daniel		Sarah	Enoch	Judaea

Worship Notes

Prayer Requests

Date:

_____

Speaker:

_____

Scriptures

Questions

Read the Bible Scriptures in Luke Chapter 24
about the resurrection of Jesus.
How many words can you spell using the letters in

RESURRECTION

_____   _____

_____   _____

_____   _____

_____   _____

_____   _____

_____   _____

_____   _____

_____   _____

Worship Notes

Date:

Questions

I can do all things through Christ which strengtheneth me. Philippians 4:13 KJV

Scriptures

Circle the words you hear in today's sermon

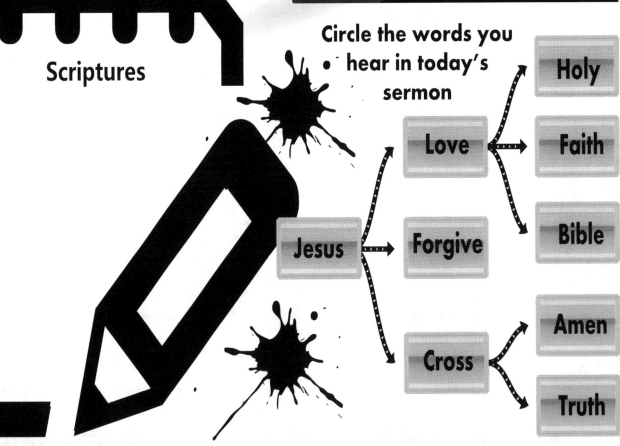

Love → Holy
Love → Faith
Jesus → Forgive → Bible
Cross → Amen
Cross → Truth

Connect the dots to reveal a butterfly and then color and decorate the wings.

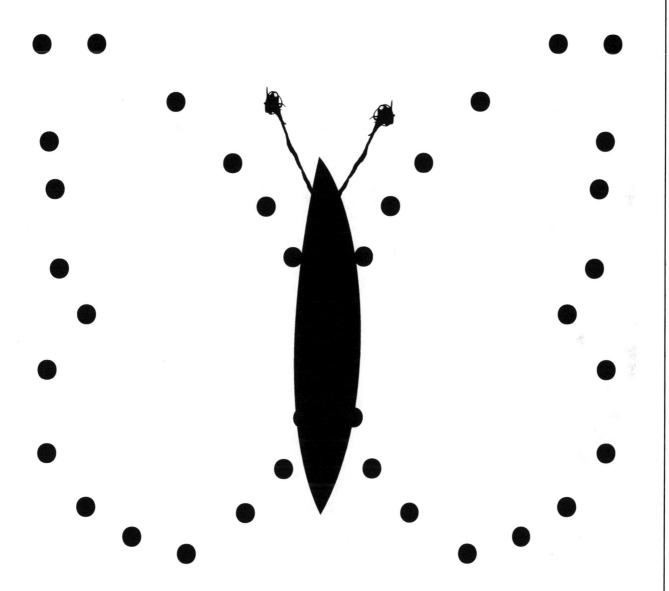

"He hath made every thing beautiful in his time."
Ecclesiastes 3:11

Worship Notes

Scripture _____

Prayer Request _____

Questions _____

FAVORITE SONG FROM TODAY'S SERVICE

IN THE BEGINNING GOD CREATED THE HEAVEN AND THE EARTH. Genesis 1:1 KJV

What is something God created?

DOODLE SPACE

HALLELUJAH

Write a description of today's sermon.
↓↓↓↓↓↓↓↓↓

Word Search

```
P U U Y K Q G G S Z S T P J U N E F U O
Z R L K C K R X A D X A H Y A Y L U W X
K O A Q T Y J B A D E K P I M W B I B O
H N C Y L A P D F Z Y Q T O S M I A O L
O D L O E P C C E O T S Q S I S B A R C
H F V H E R R N G N I A U P A Z V W E C
B E U U G Z A D G R A S A L E K C L C B
A L Y J A A Y N H J E T V Q Y O U Z A N
Z Q Q A K S E C Q J Q A A P V P R C E T
E G C L A V C N N E T V Y M W G J R I Y
L U J G I K P I M I M S I T P A B O O R
Q F W G M Z A A O L G G T N L M R S F F
U E R R F X R N A C S Y B N D A D S M Y
A O I W E G T I S Y G L U R I V I M D W
F W Z D N L Y K J B W U A U Y Z N D H V
```

BAPTISM   CHRISTIAN   FORGIVE   JESUS   PRAYER

BIBLE   CROSS   HOLY   LOVE   SALVATION

WORSHIP NOTES

DATE

SCRIPTURE

DOODLE

Your thoughts on today's sermon...

SONGS

PRAYER REQUESTS

Follow the line to discover which key unlocks the lock.

Jesus holds the key to all things.

Worship notes

How can I use my hands to be like Jesus?

Title: _____

_____

Scripture Reference: _____

_____

_____

Questions I have _____

_____

_____

For God so loved the world, that he gave his only begotten Son, that whosoever believeth in him should not perish, but have everlasting life.
John 3:16 KJV

Look up the Bible verses in your Bible and copy them in the space provided.

Proverbs 16:20

_____

_____

_____

Jeremiah 29:11

_____

_____

_____

Isaiah 53:5

_____

_____

_____

Worship Notes

Listen & Write

Words I didn't know: _____

_____

_____

Questions I have: _____

_____

_____

What I learned today: _____

_____

_____

Run to Jesus!
What can I pray for?

Today's

Date

P R A I S E   T H E   L O R D

I did that!!
Circle the word that
you did in today's service.

Today's Sermon
is found.....
Book:
Chapter:
Verse(s):

Read

Clap

Say Amen

Sing

Pray

Stand

Raise your hand(s)

Praise

Listen

Peter	Match the disciple with the paragraph that describes him.	Thomas

Peter
also known as-
Simon,
Cephas, Rock

Andrew

James
Bonerges
Son of Thunder

Judas
of Iscariot

Phillip

Nathanael
also known as-
Bartholomew

Match the disciple with the paragrah that describes him.

1.) The Bible tells nothing about this disciple expect his name. (Luke 6:15)

2.) This disciple was a fisherman on the Sea of Galilee with his father and brother.   Jesus called him to be a disciple while he was mending nets (Matthew 4:21-22). He was the first disciple to be killed for his faith (Acts 12:2).

3.) This disciple was invited to see Jesus by Philip. Jesus called him a true Israelite (John 1:45-51).

4.) This man was the keeper of the disciples' money bag. He betrayed Jesus for thirty pieces of silver (Luke 22:47-48). He was then shameful for betraying Jesus and hang himself (Matthew 27:3-5)

5.) This disciple was a fisherman with his brother on the Sea of Galilee. Jesus called him to be a disciple while he was fishing (Matthew 4:18-20). He brought his brother to Jesus (John 1:40-42).

6.) This disciple encouraged the disciples to go with Jesus and to die with Jesus (John 11:16). This doubting disciple wanted evidence that Jesus had risen from the dead, so Jesus showed him His hands and side (John 20:25-29).

7.) This disciple asked Jesus how He was going to reveal Himself to the disciples and not to the world. (John 14:22)

8.) This disciple was a fisherman with his brother on the Sea of Galilee. He walked on water to Jesus (Matthew 14:29). This disciple denied Jesus three times before His crucifixion (Luke 22:54-62).

9.) Jesus called this man to be a disciple while he was a tax collector. (Matthew 9:9)

10.) Jesus called this man to follow Him as a disciple (John 1:43-44).

11.) This disciple was a fisherman on the Sea of Galilee with his father and brother. Jesus called him to be a disciple while he was mending nets (Matthew 4:21-22). This disciple helped Peter prepare the Passover (Luke 22:8).

12.) The Bible tells nothing about this disciple expect his name. (Luke 6:15)

Thomas
also known as-
Didymus

James
son of
Alphaeus

Simon
the Zelotes

Thaddeus
also knon as-
Judas son of
James

John
Bonerges
Son of Thunder

Matthew
also known as-
Levi

Search and Find Activity

Find the pictures and color them in.
Check off each picture as you find it.

Bible Facts Quiz

Choose the correct answer for each of the questions.

1.) Who was the sister of Aaron and Moses? (Numbers 26:59)
- a. Zeruiah
- b. Tamar
- c. Miriam
- d. Abigail

2.) God stopped the sun and the moon at the request of this man. (Joshua 10:12-14)
- a. Jonadab
- b. Bildad
- c. David
- d. Joshua

3.) Jesus wept at the death of this man, and then He told him to come out of the grave. (John 11:1-44)
- a. John the Baptist
- b. Lazarus
- c. Judas
- d. Josephus

4.) Who had his foot crushed against a wall by his donkey? (Numbers 22:25)
- a. Balak
- b. Balaam
- c. Zippor
- d. Aaron

5.) Who walked on water with Jesus? (Matthew 14:25-32)
- a. Luke
- b. John
- c. Thomas
- d. Peter

6.) Who climbed a sycamore tree to see Jesus? (Luke 19:1-4)
- a. Peter
- b. Zacchaeus
- c. Noah
- d. Jason

7.) What man was healed from leprosy after dipping in the Jordan river seven times? (2 Kings 5:9-14)
- a. Naaman
- b. Matthew
- c. Peter
- d. Job

8.) Who was in prision with Paul in Pilippi? (Acts 16:25-40)
- a. Barnabas
- b. Silas
- c. Mark
- d. Timothy

9.) Who sold his birthright for a bowl of stew? (Genesis 25:29-34)
- a. Jacob
- b. Esau
- c. Judah
- d. Ishmael

10.) Who escaped from angry Jews in Damascus by being let down through a hole in the wall in a basket? (Acts 9:23-25)
- a. Silas
- b. Peter
- c. Saul
- d. Barnabas

Answers: 1-c; 2-d; 3-b; 4-b; 5-d; 6-b; 7-a; 8-b; 9-b; 10-c

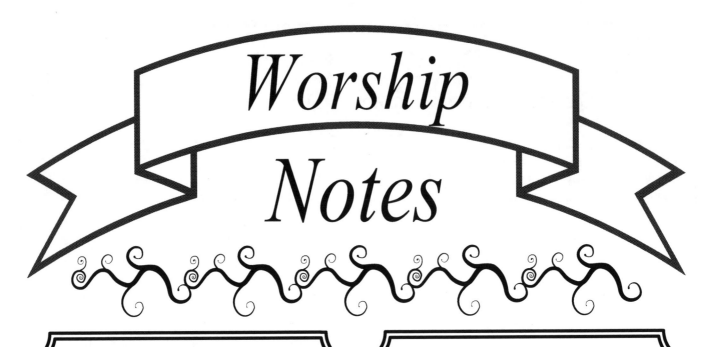

Worship Notes

Prayer Requests

Date:

Speaker:

Scriptures

Questions

In the space provided, draw a picture of a Bible story. Write out where to find the verses in the Bible.

_____

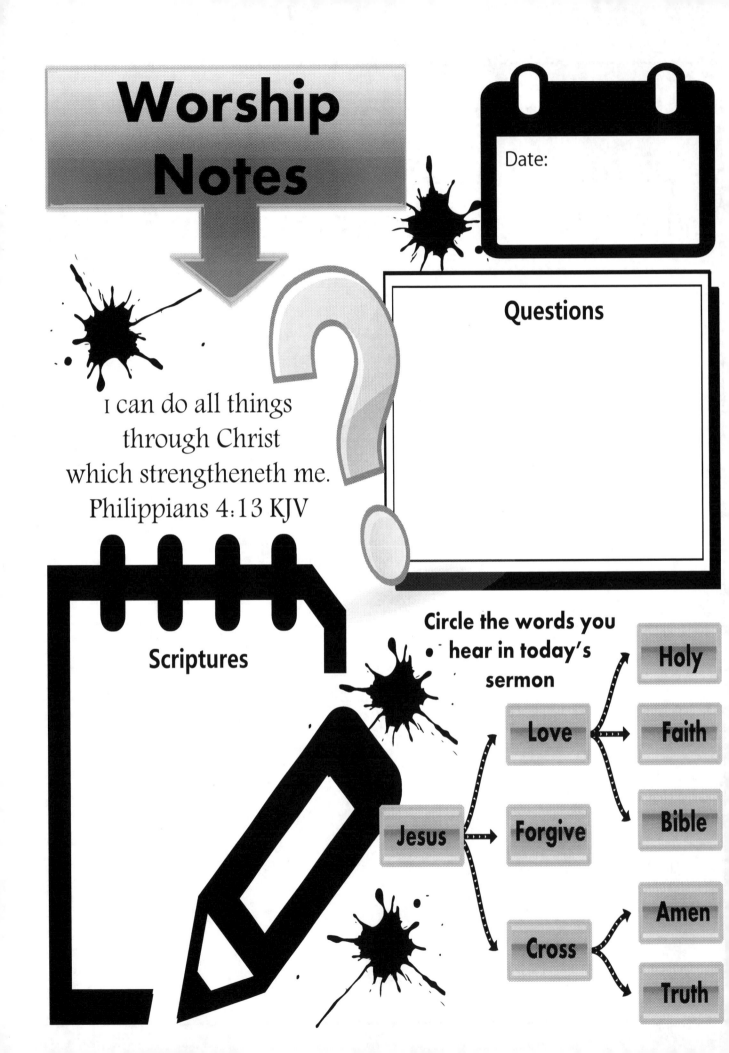

Worship Notes

I can do all things through Christ which strengtheneth me. Philippians 4:13 KJV

Date:

Questions

Scriptures

Circle the words you hear in today's sermon

Jesus

Love

Holy

Faith

Bible

Forgive

Cross

Amen

Truth

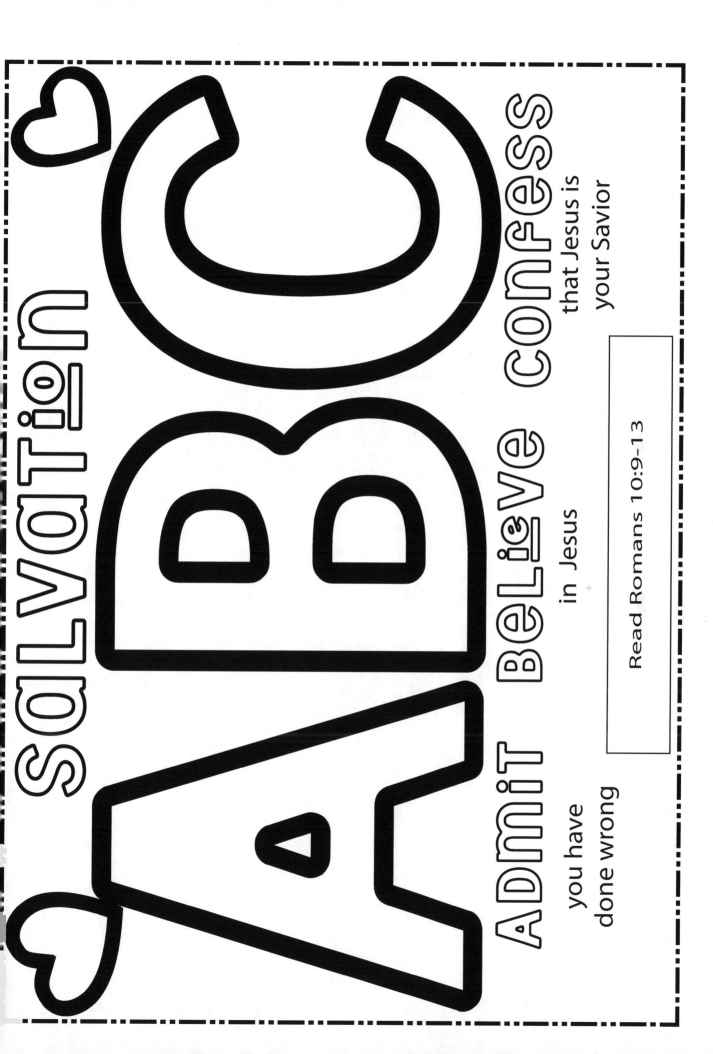

Salvation

ABC

Admit you have done wrong

Believe in Jesus

Confess that Jesus is your Savior

Read Romans 10:9-13

Worship Notes

Scripture _____

Prayer Request _____

Questions _____

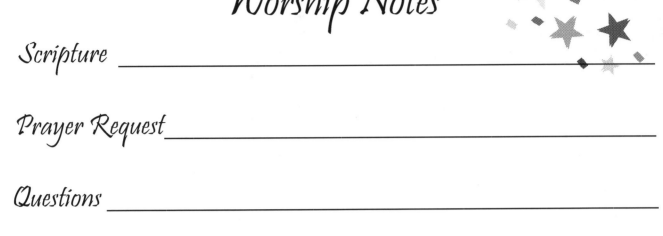

FAVORITE SONG FROM TODAY'S SERVICE

IN THE BEGINNING GOD CREATED THE HEAVEN AND THE EARTH. GENESIS 1:1 KJV

What is something God created?

DOODLE SPACE

HALLELUJAH

Write a description of today's sermon.

David & Goliath
Word Scramble

Unscramble the words and write them in the space provided.

Reference Scripture I Samuel Chapter 17

1.) NATGI

2.) ASLREI

3.) TALBTE

4.) VDAID

5.) ERSAP

6.) LISINEIPTH

7.) ROMAR

8.) LNISG HOST

9.) ILHOTGA

10.) RSDOW

Answers: 1.)Giant, 2.)Israel, 3.)Battle, 4.)David, 5.)Spear, 6.)Philistine, 7.)Armor, 8.)Sling Shot, 9.)Goliath, 10.)Sword

WORSHIP NOTES

DATE

SCRIPTURE

DOODLE

Your thoughts on today's sermon...

SONGS

PRAYER REQUESTS

HELP NOAH GET THE ANIMALS TO THE ARK BY COMPLETING THE MAZE.

"AND THE LORD SAID UNTO NOAH, COME THOU AND ALL THY HOUSE INTO THE ARK; FOR THEE HAVE I SEEN RIGHTEOUS BEFORE ME IN THIS GENERATION."
GENESIS 7:1

Worship notes

Date: _____

Speaker: _____
_____

How can I use my hands to be like Jesus?

Title: _____
_____

Scripture Reference: _____
_____
_____

Questions I have _____
_____
_____

For God so loved the world, that he gave his only begotten Son, that whosoever believeth in him should not perish, but have everlasting life.
John 3:16 KJV

Let __ __ __ __ __ thing that hath

__ __ __ __ __ __ praise the

__ __ __ __. Praise __ __ the

__ __ __ __. Psalms 150:6

A=✌   B=↵   C=👍   D=↪   E=☜   F=⇹

G=👌   H=⇇   I=🖐   J=⇈   K=☺   L=↶

M=💣   N=↪   O=🏳   P=↻   Q=✈   R=↺

S=💧   T=^   U=✝   V=▽   W=👌   X=⇧

Y=👎   Z=⇦

Worship Notes

Listen & Write

Words I didn't know: _____

_____

_____

Questions I have: _____

_____

_____

What I learned today: _____

_____

_____

Run to Jesus!
What can I pray for?

Today's

Date

PRAISE THE LORD

I did that!!
Circle the word that
you did in today's service.

Today's Sermon
is found.....
Book:
Chapter:
Verse(s):

Read

Clap

Say Amen

Sing

Pray

Stand

Raise your
hand(s)

Praise

Listen

New Testament Books

Number the New Testament books 1-27 in correct order.
For reference look at the table of contents in your Bible.

Romans	Mark	2 Timothy
Galatians	3 John	John
2 Thessalonians	Revelation	1 Corinthians
Philemon	1 Peter	James
2 John	Hebrews	Philippians
1 Timothy	Ephesians	2 Peter
Jude	2 Corinthians	Colossians
Luke	Titus	Matthew
1 John	Acts	1 Thessalonians

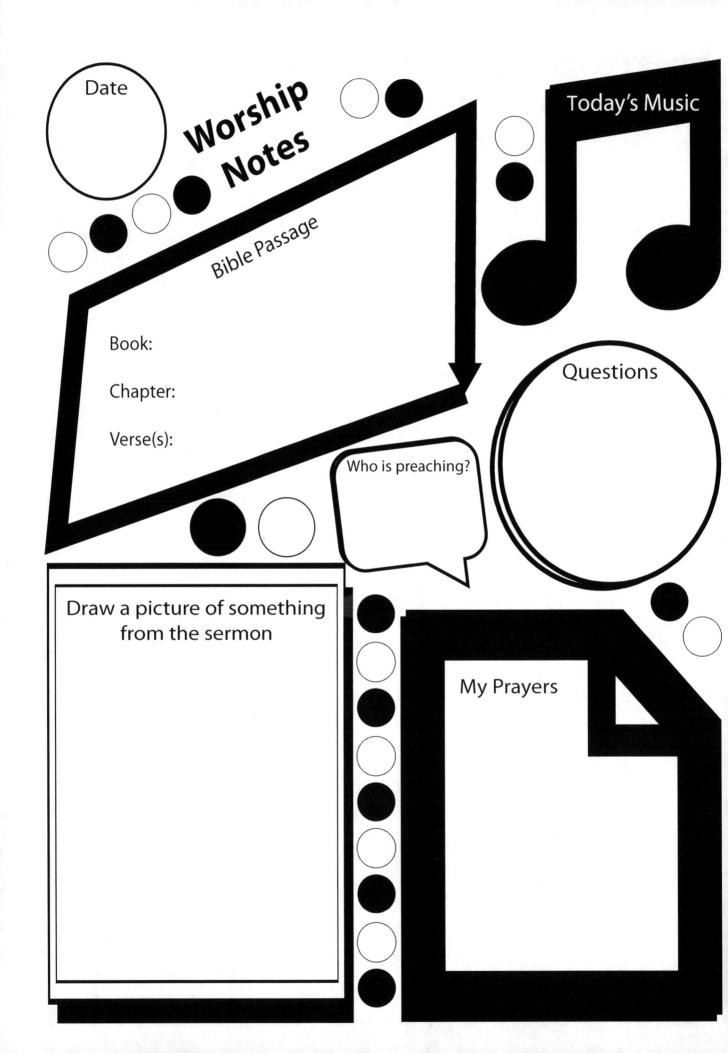

EXPLORING THE FIVE SENSES AT CHURCH

Touch

_____

_____
_____
_____
_____
_____

At church what can you...

Smell

_____
_____
_____
_____
_____

Hear

_____
_____
_____

Taste

_____
_____
_____
_____
_____
_____
_____

See

_____
_____
_____

Use the phone to decode the answers.

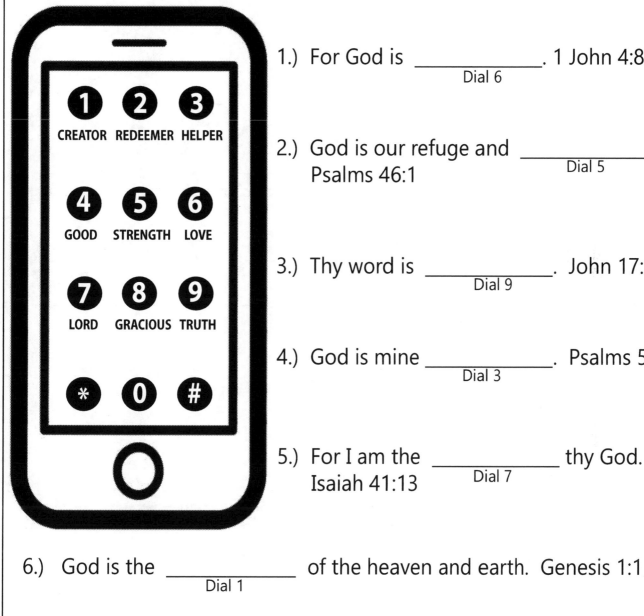

1 CREATOR **2 REDEEMER** **3 HELPER**
4 GOOD **5 STRENGTH** **6 LOVE**
7 LORD **8 GRACIOUS** **9 TRUTH**
***** **0** **#**

1.) For God is _____. 1 John 4:8
   Dial 6

2.) God is our refuge and _____.
   Psalms 46:1   Dial 5

3.) Thy word is _____. John 17:17
                Dial 9

4.) God is mine _____. Psalms 54:4
              Dial 3

5.) For I am the _____ thy God.
   Isaiah 41:13   Dial 7

6.) God is the _____ of the heaven and earth. Genesis 1:1
             Dial 1

7.) The Lord is _____ and full of compassion. Psalms 111:4
              Dial 8

8.) Oh taste and see that the Lord is _____. Psalms 34:8
                                    Dial 4

9.) As for our _____, the Lord of hosts is his name. Isaiah 47:4
             Dial 2

Worship Notes

Prayer Requests

Date: _____

Speaker: _____

Scriptures

Questions

Tic Tac Toe

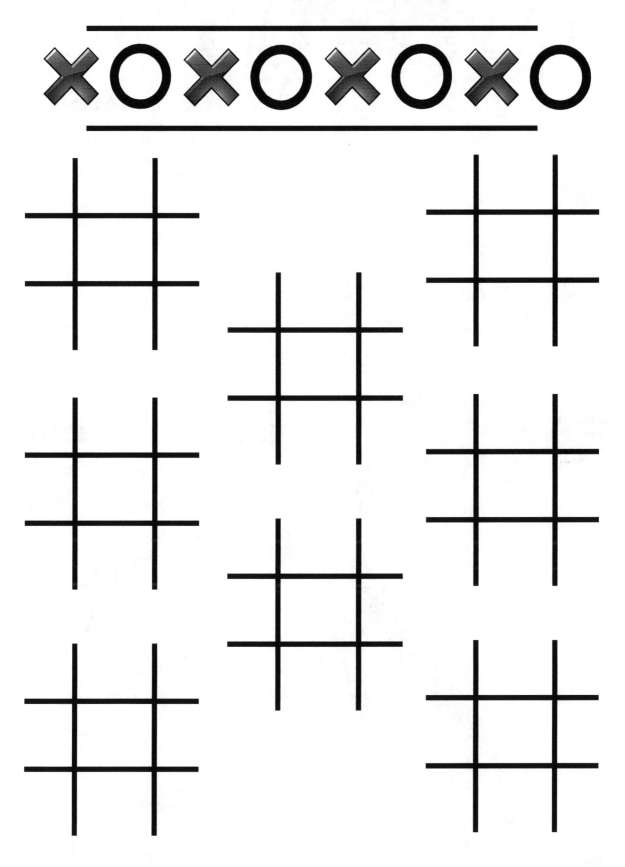

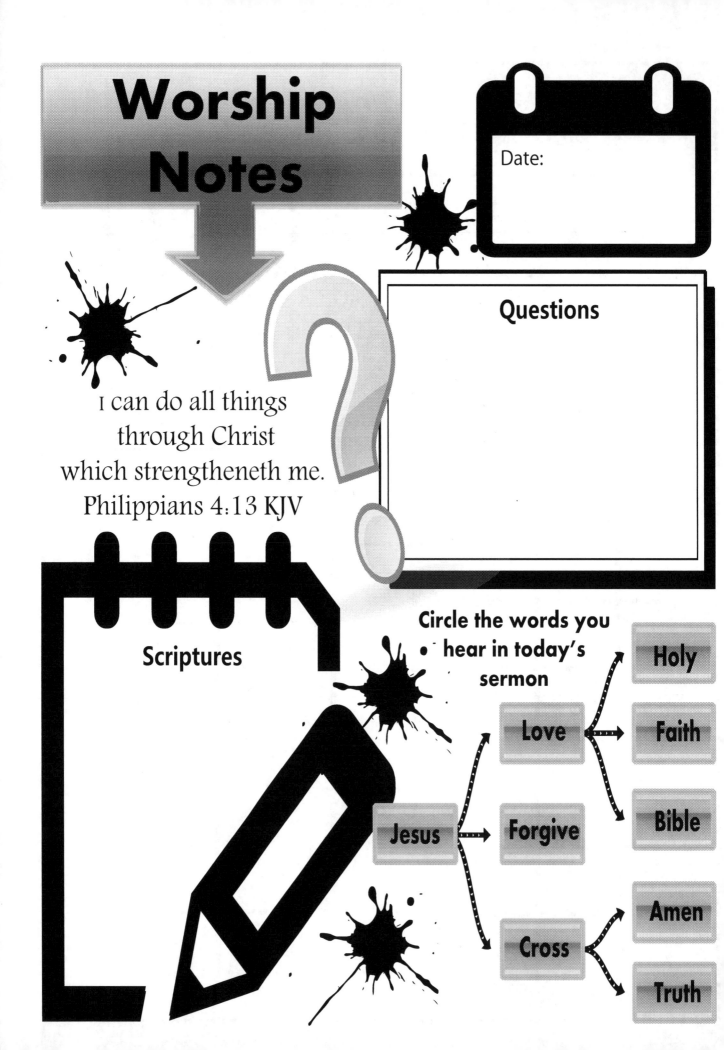

Biblical Name Alphabet Challenge
Write a name of a person in the Bible that begins with each letter in the alphabet

A_____

B_____

C_____

D_____

E_____

F_____

G_____

H_____

I_____

J_____

K_____

L_____

M_____

N_____

O_____

P_____

Q_____

R_____

S_____

T_____

U_____

V_____

W_____

X_____

Y_____

Z_____

Worship Notes

Scripture _____

Prayer Request _____

Questions _____

FAVORITE SONG FROM TODAY'S SERVICE

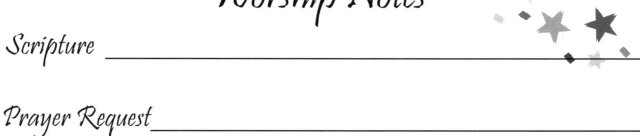

IN THE BEGINNING GOD CREATED THE HEAVEN AND THE EARTH. GENESIS 1:1 KJV

What is something God created?

HALLELUJAH

DOODLE SPACE →

Write a description of today's sermon.

Beatitude Match

Match the 'blessed are' phrase at the top to the pharse at the bottom that completes the verse. Color the two coorsponding boxes the same color. See Matthew chapter 5 for reference.

BLESSED ARE THE POOR IN SPIRIT	BLESSED ARE THE MEEK	BLESSED ARE THEY WHICH ARE PERSCUTED FOR RIGHTOUSNESS' SAKE
BLESSED ARE THE PEACEMAKERS	BLESSED ARE THE MERCIFUL	BLESSED ARE THEY THAT MOURN
BLESSED ARE THEY WHICH DO HUNGER AND THIRST AFTER RIGHTEOUSNESS	BLESSED ARE YE	BLESSED ARE THE PURE IN HEART

- -

FOR THEIRS IS THE KINGDOM OF HEAVEN	FOR THEY SHALL BE FILLED	FOR THEY SHALL INHERIT THE EARTH
FOR THEY SHALL OBTAIN MERCY	FOR THEY SHALL SEE GOD	WHEN MEN SHALL REVILE YOU, AND PERSECUTE YOU, AND SHALL SAY ALL MANNER OF EVIL AGAINST YOU FALSELY, FOR MY SAKE
FOR THEY SHALL BE COMFORTED	FOR THEY SHALL BE CALLED THE CHILDREN OF GOD	FOR THEIRS IS THE KINGDOM OF HEAVEN

WORSHIP NOTES

DATE

SCRIPTURE

DOODLE

Your thoughts on today's sermon...

SONGS

PRAYER REQUESTS

Fruit of the Spirit
Crossword Puzzle
Reference Scripture Galatians 5:22-23

Down

1.) The Fruit of the Spirit that means to be humble.
2.) The Fruit of the Spirit that means to be kind or tender.
3.) The Fruit of the Spirit that means self-control.
4.) God's _____ is grace.

Across

5.) The Fruit of the Spirit that means to be calm.
6.) The Fruit of the Spirit that means to be patient.
7.) God gives you _____ in your heart.
8.) The substance of things hoped for and the evidence of things not seen.
9.) God is _____.

Word Bank
- Love
- Joy
- Peace
- Longsuffering
- Gentleness
- Goodness
- Faith
- Meekness
- Temperance

Worship NOTES

How can I use my hands to be like Jesus?

Title: _____

_____

Scripture Reference: _____

_____

_____

Questions I have _____

_____

_____

For God so loved the world, that he gave his only begotten Son, that whosoever believeth in him should not perish, but have everlasting life.
John 3:16 KJV

Color the path from Jesus to the cross red to symbolize the blood He shed for us.

"In whom we have redemption through his blood, the forgiveness of sins, according to the riches of his grace;"
Ephesians 1:7

Worship Notes

Listen & Write

Words I didn't know: _____

_____

_____

Questions I have: _____

_____

_____

What I learned today: _____

_____

_____

Run to Jesus!
What can I pray for?

Today's

Date

PRAISE THE LORD

I did that!!
Circle the word that
you did in today's service.

Today's Sermon
is found.....
Book:
Chapter:
Verse(s):

Read

Clap

Say Amen

Sing

Pray

Stand

Raise your hand(s)

Praise

Listen

Look up the Bible verse in your Bible
and fill in the missing words in the blanks provided.

(Scriptures taken from the KJV, wording in other versions may vary.)

Fear thou not; for I am _____ thee: be not
dismayed; for I am thy God: I will
_____ thee; yea, I will _____ thee;
yea, I will _____ thee with the right hand
of my _____. Isaiah 41:10

Now _____ is the _____ of things
_____ for, the _____ of things not
seen. Hebrews 11:1

Be still, and _____ that I am God: I will be
_____ among the heathen, I will be
_____ in the earth. Psalms 46:10

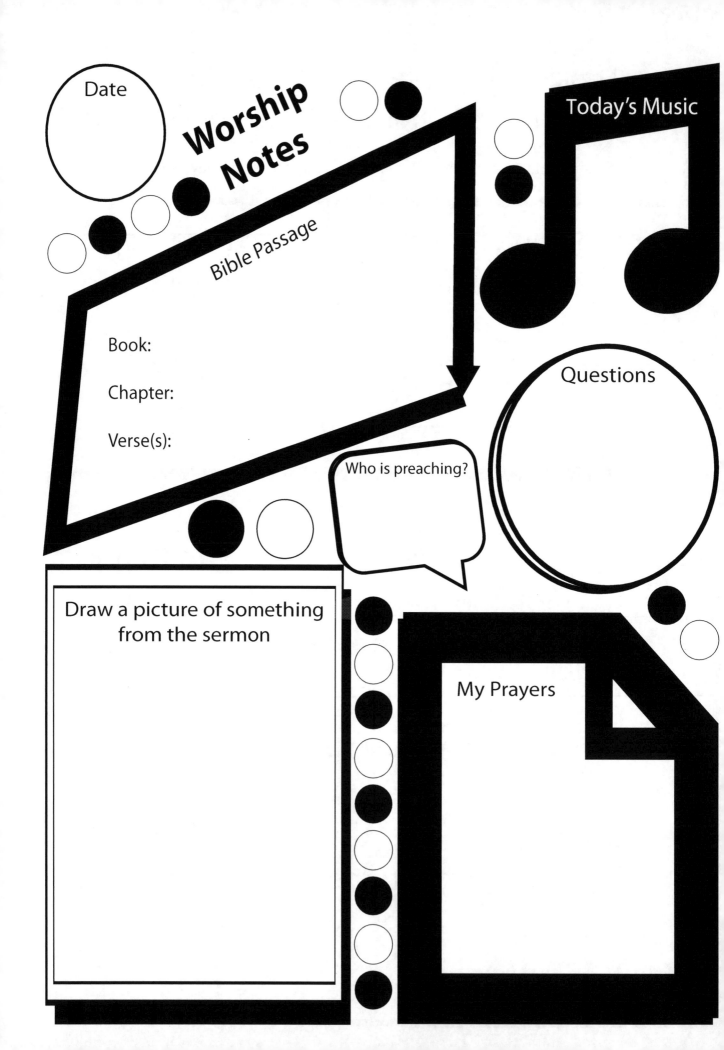

What did God create
on each day?
Draw a line from the Day to what
God created on that day.
For reference you can read Genesis Chapter 1

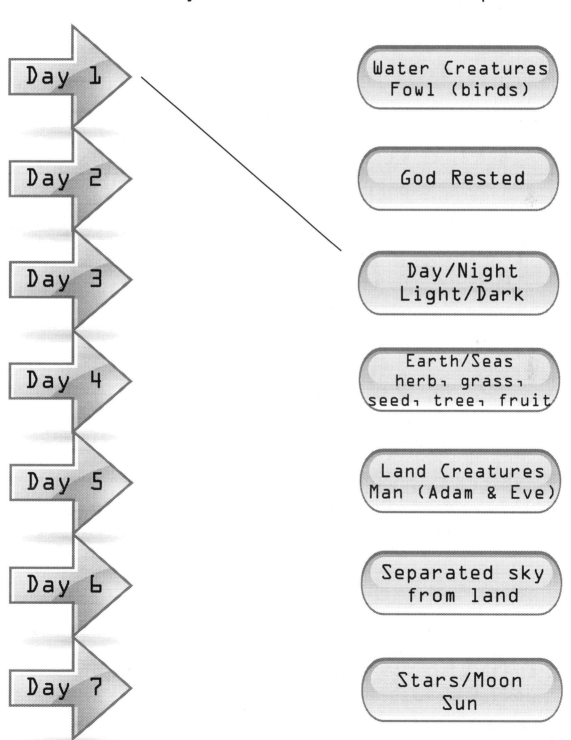

Day 1

Day 2

Day 3

Day 4

Day 5

Day 6

Day 7

Water Creatures
Fowl (birds)

God Rested

Day/Night
Light/Dark

Earth/Seas
herb, grass,
seed, tree, fruit

Land Creatures
Man (Adam & Eve)

Separated sky
from land

Stars/Moon
Sun

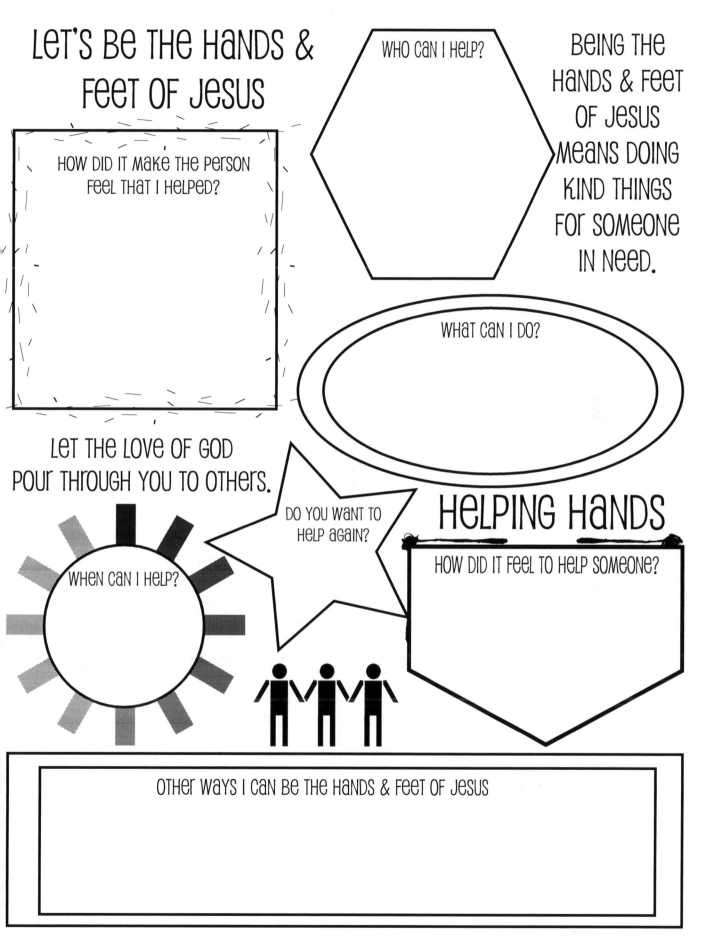

LET'S BE THE HANDS & FEET OF JESUS

WHO CAN I HELP?

BEING THE HANDS & FEET OF JESUS MEANS DOING KIND THINGS FOR SOMEONE IN NEED.

HOW DID IT MAKE THE PERSON FEEL THAT I HELPED?

WHAT CAN I DO?

LET THE LOVE OF GOD POUR THROUGH YOU TO OTHERS.

DO YOU WANT TO HELP AGAIN?

HELPING HANDS

HOW DID IT FEEL TO HELP SOMEONE?

WHEN CAN I HELP?

OTHER WAYS I CAN BE THE HANDS & FEET OF JESUS

BE A BLESSING

Worship Notes

Prayer Requests

Date: _____

Speaker: _____

Scriptures

Questions

TEN COMMANDMENTS
Fill in the blanks using words from the word bank. For help look up the reference scripture Exodus 20:1-17.

1.) You shall have no _____ gods before me.

2.) You shall not make unto thee any _____ images.

3.) You shall not take the _____ of the Lord thy God in vain.

4.) Remember the _____ day to keep it holy.

5.) _____ your father and your mother.

6.) You _____ not kill.

7.) You shall not _____ adultery.

8.) You shall not _____.

9.) You shall not bear false witness against your _____.

10.) You shall not _____ your neighbor's goods.

Word Bank

graven	commit	steal	neighbor	shall
name	covet	honor	other	Sabbath

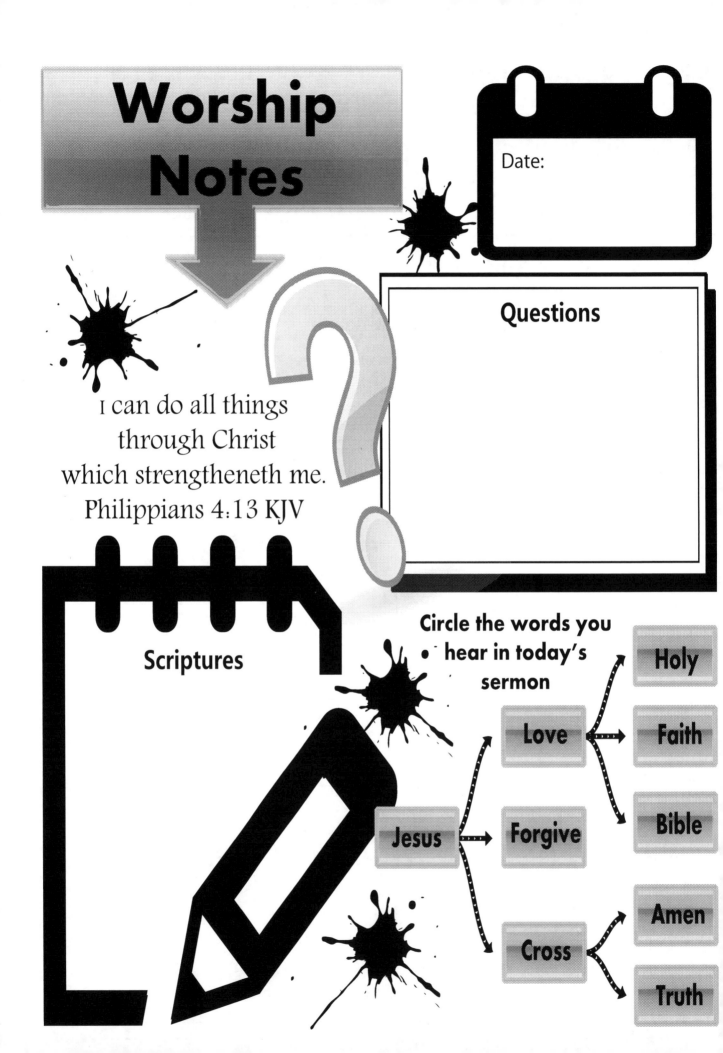

The Holy Bible is a precious book that guides us in how we should follow Jesus.
How many words can you spell using the letters in

HOLY BIBLE

_____   _____

_____   _____

_____   _____

_____   _____

_____   _____

_____   _____

_____   _____

_____   _____

Worship Notes

Scripture _____

Prayer Request _____

Questions _____

FAVORITE SONG FROM TODAY'S SERVICE

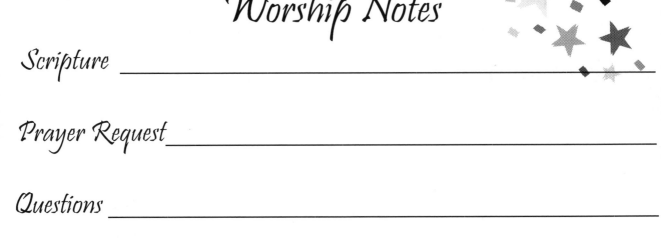

IN THE BEGINNING GOD CREATED THE HEAVEN AND THE EARTH. GENESIS 1:1 KJV

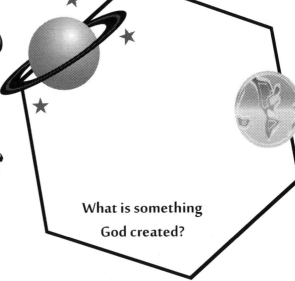

What is something God created?

DOODLE SPACE

HALLELUJAH

Write a description of today's sermon.

Search and Find Activity

Find the pictures and color them in.
Check off each picture as you find it.

WORSHIP NOTES

DATE

SCRIPTURE

DOODLE

Your thoughts on today's sermon...

SONGS

PRAYER REQUESTS

Word Search

```
L C P P F P F I S V A M D S X R O Q U E
T A A T R V M U D B D Z I W J N D Q S V
N T X X R O E J I A E S S Y H F Z I S H
Q Y R L A A J G H B L F I S W D B C Y L
S Q B N H B A I X K I X F S X P T T P T
S N H C T I R U T H L X T J A N Q Q T G
N D C B L A M Q K P A A A L F A X H K D
W A D R C A Z Q F W H M A C L V C W T Y
Z E J W F P I G E P E E N J J D J W U E
M B Y Z K A Q O F S Q G W B H A P X Q X
N M D H H B Q P X X T R U E P J A U X
B N X T Y B I E E I R S Y I J A G B H F
G Q R F R K U A R L V W N B S W Q L O W
I A P E T E R J C P I D U W X M S G D S
M H Y L H N Q G I F D C U Z G U Y N O E
M R Q M G Q O Q F S P X K I M I S G H E
V J U I O Q A B H O W D W S C E N Z V
L J Y W Z I N Y O F D E I Z S Q D S C
P H X H A F Q B L B O V D E F Q E V D S
A N T D D G G N N N U V I O L X M K H K
```

PETER	JAMES	GIDEON	ISAAC	ZACCHAEUS

ABIGAIL	DELILAH	MARTHA	RUTH	NAOMI

Worship notes

How can I use my hands to be like Jesus?

Title: _____

_____

Scripture Reference: _____

_____

_____

Questions I have _____

_____

_____

For God so loved the world, that he gave his only begotten Son, that whosoever believeth in him should not perish, but have everlasting life.
John 3:16 KJV

Follow the line to discover which key unlocks the lock.

Jesus holds the key to all things.

Worship Notes

Listen & Write

Words I didn't know: _____

_____

_____

Questions I have: _____

_____

_____

What I learned today: _____

_____

_____

Run to Jesus!
What can I pray for?

Today's

Date

PRAISE THE LORD

I did that!!
Circle the word that
you did in today's service.

Today's Sermon
is found.....
Book:
Chapter:
Verse(s):

Read

Clap

Say Amen

Sing

Pray

Stand

Raise your
hand(s)

Praise

Listen

Look up the Bible verses in your Bible and copy them in the space provided.

Ephesians 4:29

_____

_____

_____

2 Corinthians 12:9

_____

_____

_____

Matthew 17:20

_____

_____

_____

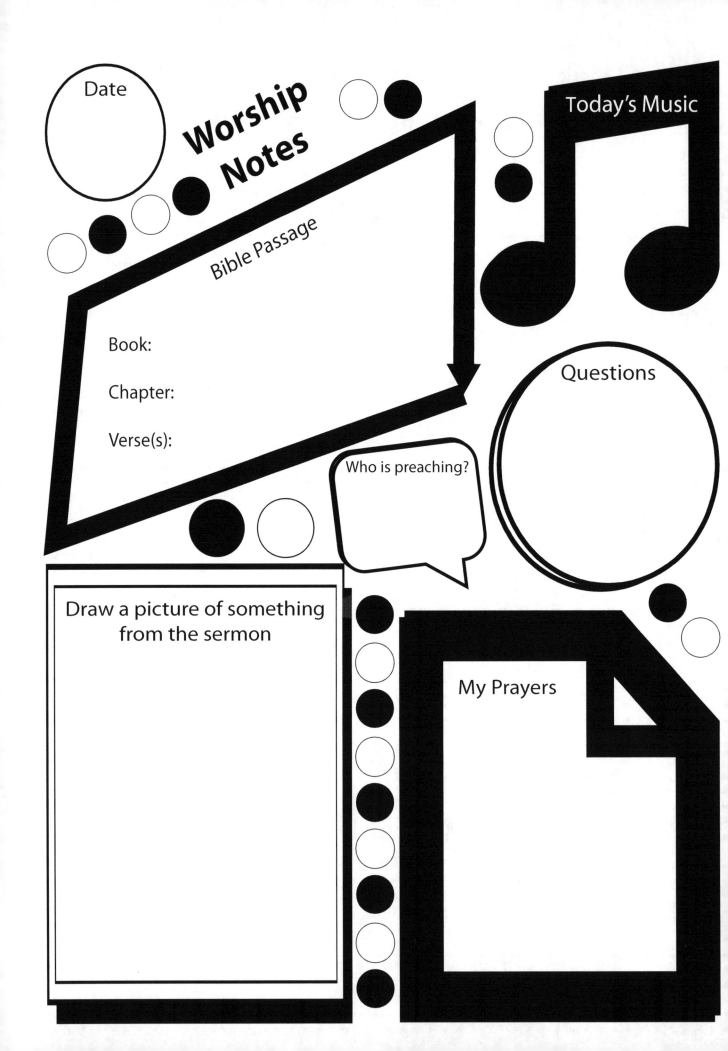

THE ARMOR OF GOD
DRAW A LINE FROM THE PIECE OF ARMOR TO IT'S DESCRIPTION
REFERENCE SCRIPTURE EPHESIANS 6:10-20

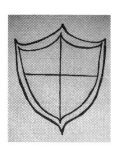

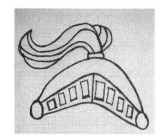

Sheild of Faith:
The sheild of faith stops all the devil's tricks from hitting you.

Breastplate of Righteousness:
The breatplate of righteousness protects your heart to keep it pure and full of Christ.

Helmet of Salvation:
Knowing that you are saved and keeping your mind set on Jesus protects you.

Shoes of the Gospel of Peace:
Always be ready to share Jeaus and His peace wherever you go.

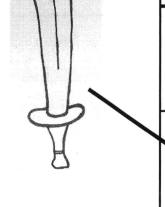

Sword of the Spirit:
God's Word (the Bible) is the sword of the Spirit. Learn it and speak it with boldness.

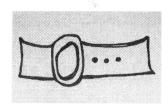

Belt of Truth:
Jeus is the truth, so wearing the belt of truth allows Jesus to protect you from the devil.

Praying Hands:
Prayer is your communication with God and how you grow your relationship with Him.

"Finally, my brethren, be strong in the Lord, and in the power of his might. Put on the whole armour of God, that ye may be able to stand against the wiles of the devil." Ephesians 6:10-11

The Five Finger Prayer

An easy way to remember those to include in your prayer.

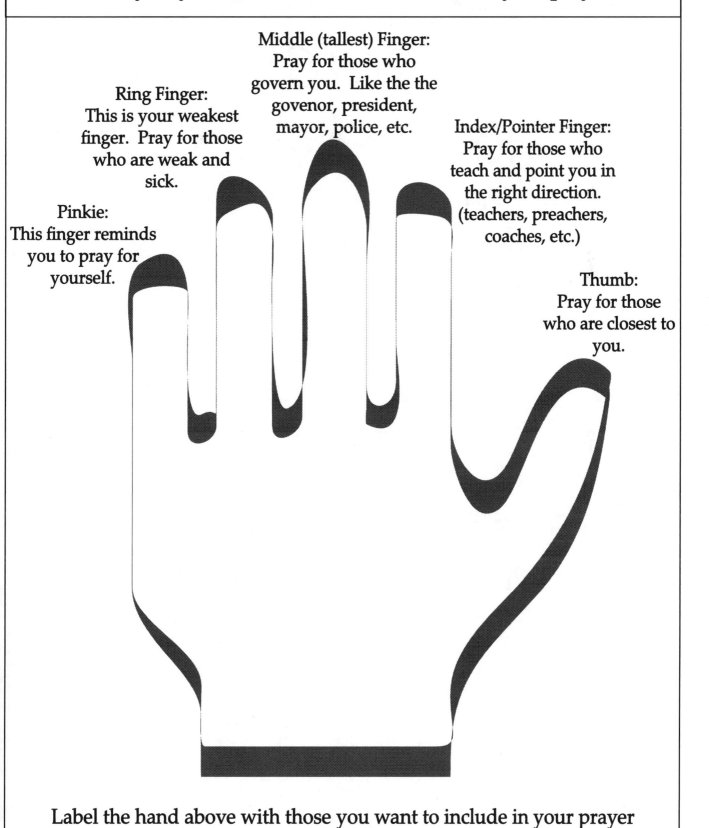

Middle (tallest) Finger:
Pray for those who
govern you. Like the the
govenor, president,
mayor, police, etc.

Ring Finger:
This is your weakest
finger. Pray for those
who are weak and
sick.

Index/Pointer Finger:
Pray for those who
teach and point you in
the right direction.
(teachers, preachers,
coaches, etc.)

Pinkie:
This finger reminds
you to pray for
yourself.

Thumb:
Pray for those
who are closest to
you.

Label the hand above with those you want to include in your prayer

Worship Notes

Prayer Requests

Date:

Speaker:

Scriptures

Questions

Categories of the books of the Bible.
Fill in the missing letters of the Bible book title to complete each list.
Use your Bible index for reference.

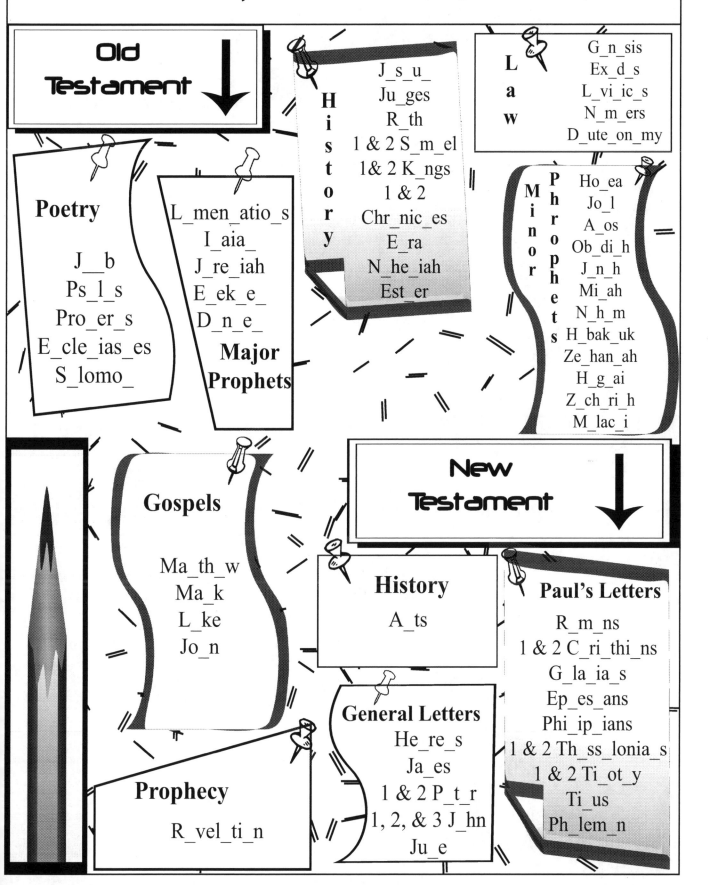

Old Testament ↓

Law
G_n_sis
Ex_d_s
L_vi_ic_s
N_m_ers
D_ute_on_my

History
J_s_u_
Ju_ges
R_th
1 & 2 S_m_el
1 & 2 K_ngs
1 & 2 Chr_nic_es
E_ra
N_he_iah
Est_er

Poetry
J__b
Ps_l_s
Pro_er_s
E_cle_ias_es
S_lomo_

L_men_atio_s
I_aia_
J_re_iah
E_ek_e_
D_n_e_
Major Prophets

Minor Prophets
Ho_ea
Jo_l
A_os
Ob_di_h
J_n_h
Mi_ah
N_h_m
H_bak_uk
Ze_han_ah
H_g_ai
Z_ch_ri_h
M_lac_i

Gospels
Ma_th_w
Ma_k
L_ke
Jo_n

New Testament ↓

History
A_ts

Paul's Letters
R_m_ns
1 & 2 C_ri_thi_ns
G_la_ia_s
Ep_es_ans
Phi_ip_ians
1 & 2 Th_ss_lonia_s
1 & 2 Ti_ot_y
Ti_us
Ph_lem_n

General Letters
He_re_s
Ja_es
1 & 2 P_t_r
1, 2, & 3 J_hn
Ju_e

Prophecy
R_vel_ti_n

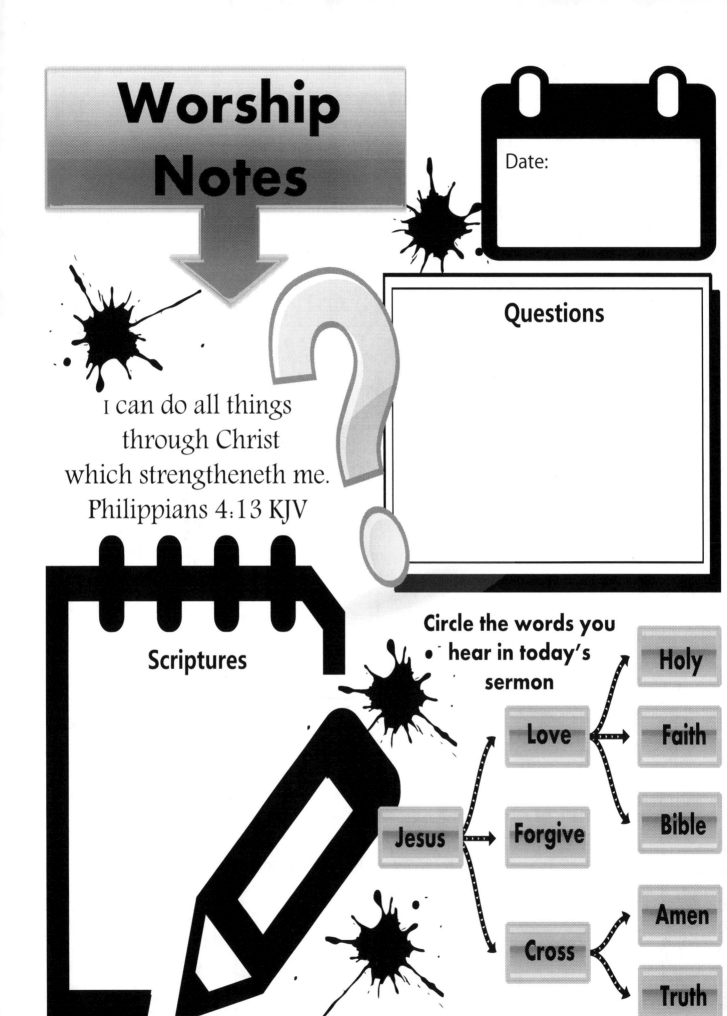

In the space provided write a letter to God.

_____

_____

_____

_____

_____

_____

_____

_____

_____

_____

Worship Notes

Scripture _____

Prayer Request _____

Questions _____

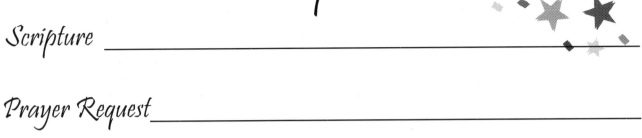

IN THE BEGINNING GOD CREATED THE HEAVEN AND THE EARTH. GENESIS 1:1 KJV

FAVORITE SONG FROM TODAY'S SERVICE

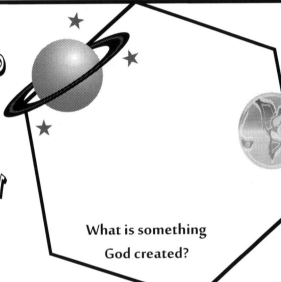

What is something God created?

DOODLE SPACE

HALLELUJAH

Write a description of today's sermon.

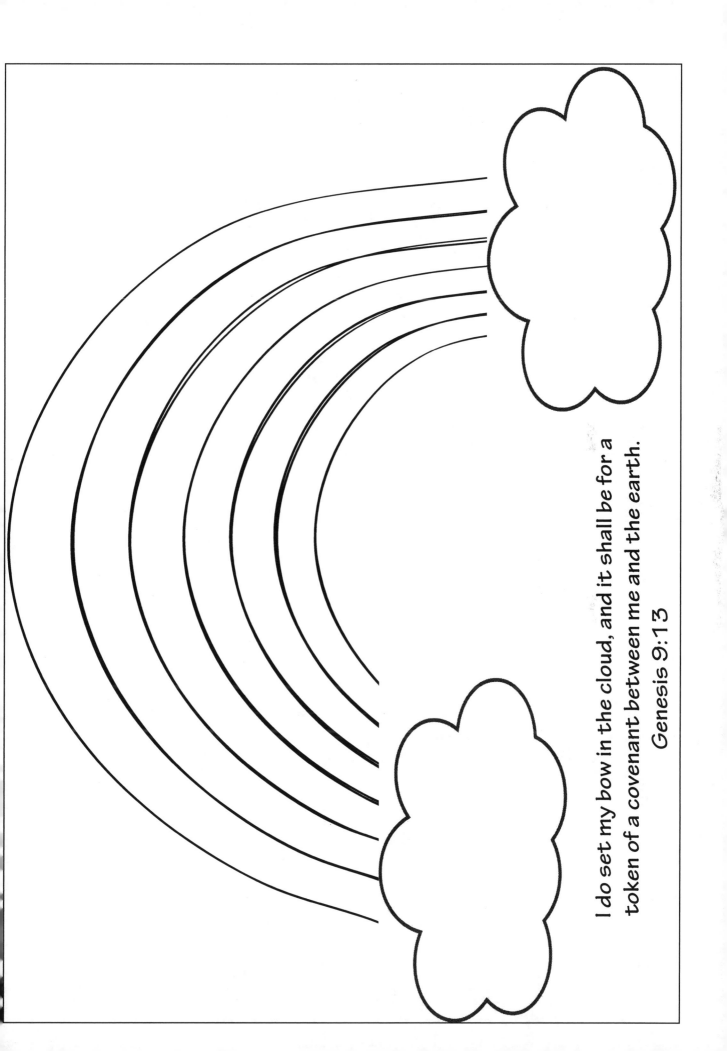

I do set my bow in the cloud, and it shall be for a token of a covenant between me and the earth.

Genesis 9:13

WORSHIP NOTES

DATE

SCRIPTURE

DOODLE

Your thoughts on today's sermon...

SONGS

PRAYER REQUESTS

Shadrach, Meshach, & Abednego Word Scramble

Unscramble the words and write them in the space provided.

Reference Scripture Daniel Chapter 3

1.) ZNBREHUDAENACZ

2.) YIRFE

3.) THO

4.) DAHCAHSR

5.) HASHEMC

6.) URFO NEM

7.) SEUSJ

8.) ENURACF

9.) GEBANODE

10.) DOGL

Worship notes

*How can I use my hands
to be like Jesus?*

Title: _____

_____

Scripture Reference: _____

_____

_____

Questions I have _____

_____

_____

For God so loved the
world, that he gave
his only begotten Son,
that whosoever
believeth in him should
not perish, but have
everlasting life.
John 3:16 KJV

HELP THE BIRD FLY THROUGH THE MAZE TO GET TO THE FOREST.

"...YE ARE OF MORE VALUE THAN MANY SPARROWS." MATTHEW 10:31

Worship Notes

Listen & Write

Words I didn't know: _____

_____

_____

Questions I have: _____

_____

_____

What I learned today: _____

_____

_____

Run to Jesus!
What can I pray for?

Today's

Date

PRAISE THE LORD

I did that!!
Circle the word that
you did in today's service.

Today's Sermon
is found.....
Book:
Chapter:
Verse(s):

Read

Clap

Say Amen

Sing

Pray

Stand

Raise your hand(s)

Praise

Listen

Use the key to fill in the blanks and
complete the Bible verse.
(verses taken from the KJV)

Jesus __ __ __ __ __ __ the same

__ __ __ __ __ __ __ __ __ , and to

__ __ __ , and for __ __ __ __ .

Hebrews 13:8

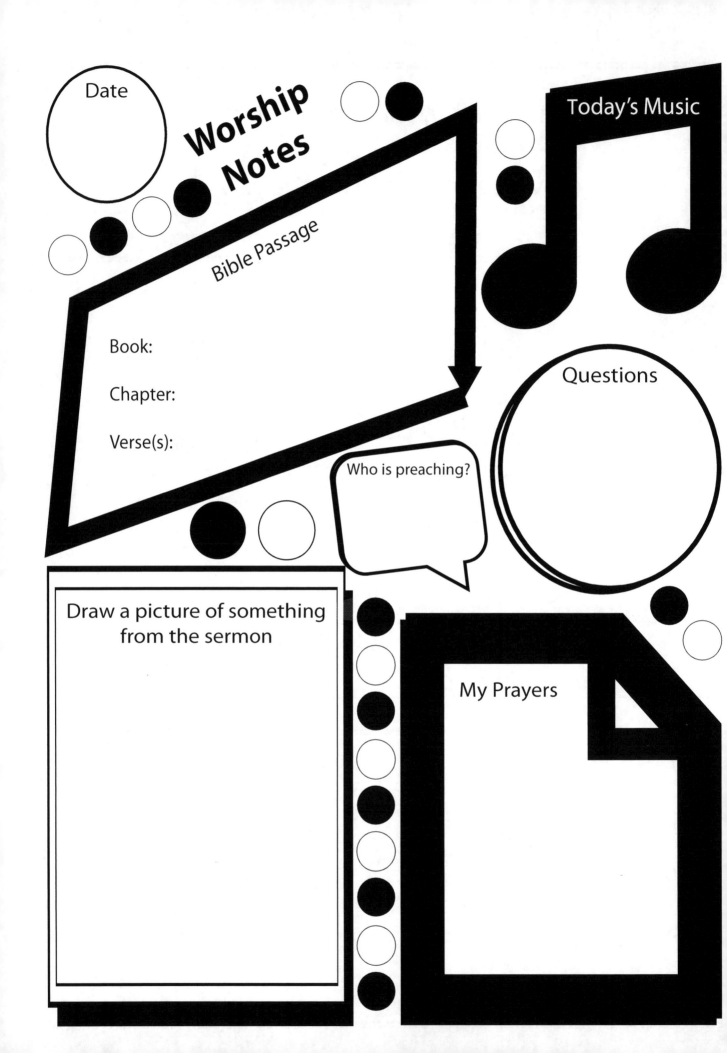

Old Testament Books

Number the Old Testament books 1-39 in correct order.

For reference look at the table of contents in your Bible.

Malachi	Hosea	Psalms
Esther	Ecclesiastes	Judges
2 Kings	Job	2 Chronicles
Nehemiah	Lamentations	Solomon
Proverbs	Ezra	Micah
Leviticus	Zechariah	1 Samuel
Ruth	Joshua	Amos
Genesis	1 Kings	Jeremiah
Ezekiel	Isaiah	Exodus
Numbers	Habakkuk	Zephaniah
Joel	Jonah	Daniel
1 Chronicles	Deuteronomy	Obadiah
Nahum	2 Samuel	Haggai

Prayer Requests

Today's Scriptures

Words I did
not understand

RAISE YOUR HANDS!

SHOUT AMEN!

JESUS IS THE KING!

Songs

Doodles
&
Thoughts

Write what you
are thankful for...

Worship Notes

God is Good

TESTIFY

God is so
good!!

In the spaces
provided write
the good news of
what God has
done for you!

Worship Notes

Prayer Requests

Date:

_____

Speaker:

_____

Scriptures

Questions

Bible Facts Quiz

Choose the correct answer for each of the questions.

1.) What is the first book in the Old Testament?
- a.) Leviticus
- b.) Obadiah
- c.) Ecclesiastes
- d.) Genesis

2.) What is the longest book in the Bible?
- a.) Proverbs
- b.) Matthew
- c.) Psalms
- d.) Revelation

3.) What is the first book in the New Testament?
- a.) Matthew
- b.) Philippians
- c.) Mark
- d.) 1 Peter

4.) What is the shortest verse in the Bible?
- a.) Isaiah 11:16
- b.) Galatians 4:31
- c.) Ezekiel 4:17
- d.) John 11:35

5.) What is the longest chapter in the Bible?
- a.) Psalms 119
- b.) Genesis 1
- c.) Luke 24
- d.) Leviticus 14

6.) What is the last book in the New Testament?
- a.) Romans
- b.) Titus
- c.) Revelation
- d.) Jude

7.) What is the shortest book in the Bible
- a.) 1 John
- b.) 2 John
- c.) 3 John
- d.) St. John

8.) What is the last book in the Old Testament?
- a.) Malachi
- b.) Nahum
- c.) Micah
- d.) Nehemiah

9.) What is the shortest chapter in the Bible?
- a.) Revelation 15
- b.) Exodus 4
- c.) 1 Thessalonians 1
- d.) Psalms 117

10.) What is the longest verse in the Bible?
- a.) James 4:1
- b.) Esther 8:9
- c.) Romans 15:6
- d.) Jeremiah 44:12

Answers: 1-d; 2-c; 3-a; 4-d; 5-a; 6-c; 7-c; 8-a; 9-d; 10-b

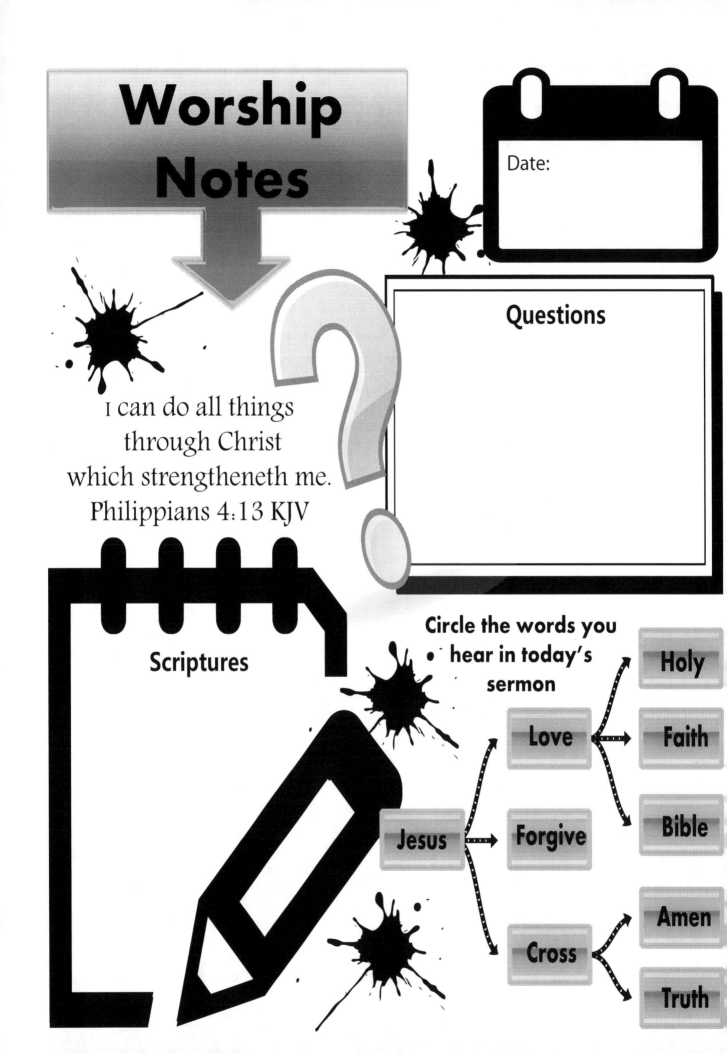

Biblical Alphabet Challenge
Write the name of something in the Bible that begins with each letter in the alphabet

A_____

B_____

C_____

D_____

E_____

F_____

G_____

H_____

I_____

J_____

K_____

L_____

M_____

N_____

O_____

P_____

Q_____

R_____

S_____

T_____

U_____

V_____

W_____

X_____

Y_____

Z_____

Worship Notes

Scripture _____

Prayer Request _____

Questions _____

FAVORITE SONG FROM TODAY'S SERVICE

IN THE BEGINNING GOD CREATED THE HEAVEN AND THE EARTH. GENESIS 1:1 KJV

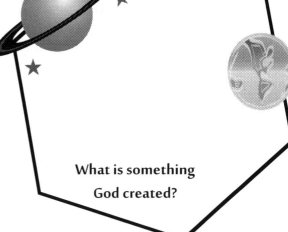

What is something God created?

DOODLE SPACE →

HALLELUJAH

Write a description of today's sermon.

Tic Tac Toe

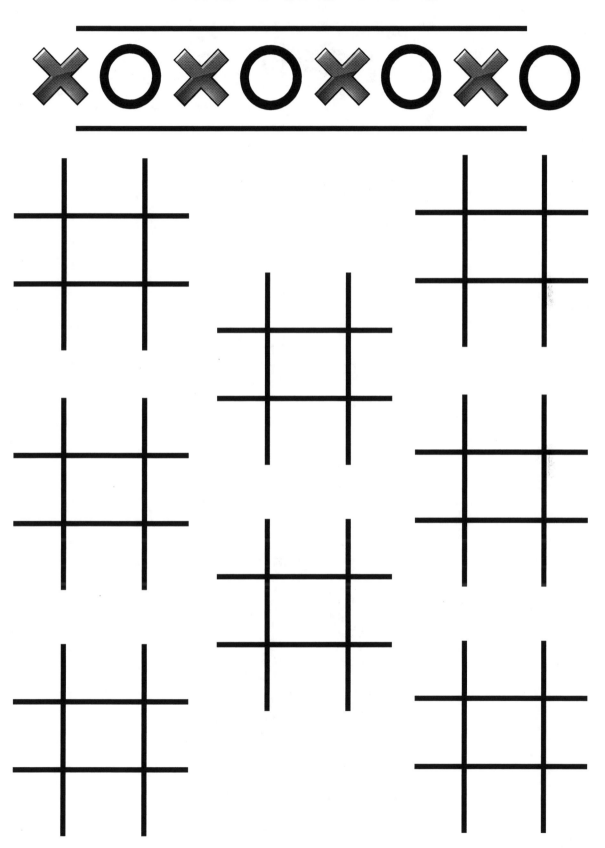

WORSHIP NOTES

DATE

SCRIPTURE

DOODLE

Your thoughts on today's sermon...

SONGS

PRAYER REQUESTS

Let's play Bingo.

Look around the church and mark the card with what you see.
Five in a row is bingo. Try and fill the whole card.

B I N G O

B	I	N	G	O
Someone Wearing a Flower	Bible	Something Red	Cross	Someone Wearing Brown Shoes
Teacher	Someone Wearing a Suit	Someone Smiling	A Baby Drinking From a Bottle	Altar
People Hugging	Piano	Free Space	Annoiting Oil	Someone Wearing the Color Purple
Song Book	Someone Saying Amen	Someone Praying	Someone Wearing Glasses	Preacher
Family With Five Children	Guitar	Tissue Box	Drums	The Word Love

Worship

NOTES

Date: _____

Speaker: _____
_____

How can I use my hands
to be like Jesus?

Title: _____

_____

Scripture Reference: _____

_____

_____

*Questions I have*_____

_____

_____

For God so loved the
world, that he gave
his only begotten Son,
that whosoever
believeth in him should
not perish, but have
everlasting life.
John 3:16 KJV

Printed in the United States
By Bookmasters